Stop That Germ

by Rod Barkman

BEARPORT
PUBLISHING

Minneapolis, Minnesota

Credits

All images are courtesy of Shutterstock.com, unless otherwise specified. With thanks to Getty Images, Thinkstock Photo, and iStockphoto.
Cover – Svetlana Shamshurina. Recurring – ONYXprj, robuart, Anatolir. 4 – Lomonovskyi. 5 – Tartila. 6 – Golden Vector, Dr_Microbe. 7 – spanteldotru, nopparit. 8 – YuliiaDU. 11 – Elegant Solution, Dzm1try, thanya, simonkr, New Africa, Phynart Studio. 12 – Yuliia Konakhovska, Michael Burrell. 14–15 – ONYXprj. 16–17 – elenabsl. 18 – ONYXprj. 19 – hvostik, Sylfida. 20 – Maike Hildebrandt. 21 – hvostik. 22 – matsabe, Neliakott, StockPhotosArt, clubfoto. 23 – Sylfida, VioletaStoimenova.

Library of Congress Cataloging-in-Publication Data is available at www.loc.gov or upon request from the publisher.

ISBN: 979-8-88916-973-4 (hardcover)
ISBN: 979-8-89232-495-3 (paperback)
ISBN: 979-8-89232-135-8 (ebook)

© 2025 BookLife Publishing
This edition is published by arrangement with BookLife Publishing.

For more information, write to Bearport Publishing, 5357 Penn Avenue South, Minneapolis, MN 55419.

Contents

Too Small to See

What is the smallest thing you can think of? Draw it on a piece of paper. Can you imagine something even smaller?

Germs are so itty-bitty that we can't spot them with our eyes alone. Yet, they are around us all the time!

Meet the Germs

Let's meet three main types of germs.

Nice to meet you! I'm a **fungus**. Some of my fungi friends are nice, but others are troublemakers.

Hi, I'm a **bacterium** (bak-TEER-ee-uhm). Just like fungi, most of my bacteria friends are good . . . but some cause problems!

Hello! I'm a **virus**. Sorry, but viruses and humans don't usually get along.

Making Me Sick

Most germs around us are safe, but some can be bad for us. If bad germs get into our bodies, they make us feel sick.

Bad germs can make our throats hurt. They can also make us cough or sneeze.

Have you ever had a **cold**? Sorry, that was because of one of us viruses!

COUGH! COUGH!

Getting Around

Germs can **spread** in many ways. Let's learn some of them!

Air

When we cough or sneeze, germs shoot from our bodies and into the air. *Wheee!*

Surfaces

Germs can move place to place on our hands, clothes, and even our pets!

Water

Some germs can travel place to place in water.

Touch

Germs can move between people when they touch each other.

Cover Up

Many germs travel through the air. How can we stop them?

Cover your mouth and nose with a tissue before you cough or sneeze.

Tissues help catch germs when we cough or sneeze. But what about when we breathe?

Wear a mask that covers your nose and mouth. This helps stop germs from getting into the air.

A mask

Super Soap

From high fives to handshakes, germs can spread in many different ways. Luckily, there is an easy way to keep bad germs from being passed along . . . by washing our hands!

It is very important to wash our hands often.

Washing your hands with warm water and soap will get rid of most bad germs.

Don't forget to clean under your fingernails, too!

Step by Step

Follow these simple steps for washing your hands!

1 Wet your hands, and put soap on them.

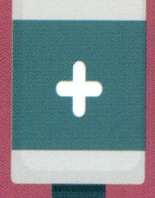

2 Rub soap between your hands.

3 Wash the backs of your hands.

4 Clean between your fingers.

5 Lock your fingers together, then rub your fingertips.

6 Rub both thumbs.

7 Wash the palms of your hands again.

8 Rinse the soap off with water.

9 Dry your hands with a towel.

Did you know?

Using the towel to turn off the tap will keep your hands cleaner!

17

Sparkling Clean

Any **surface** you touch often has germs. Germs can stay on surfaces for a long time. When we touch them, the germs get on us.

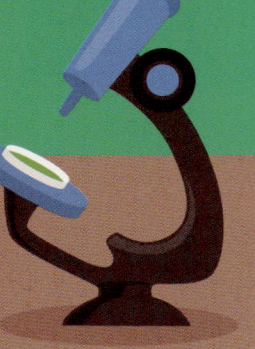

Luckily, there are ways to make anything you touch safer.

Spray a surface with a cleaner. Let the cleaner sit for a little bit. Then, wipe it off with a towel. This will get rid of most germs.

Safe Water

Humans, animals, and plants need water to **survive**. But water can carry germs that can make us sick.

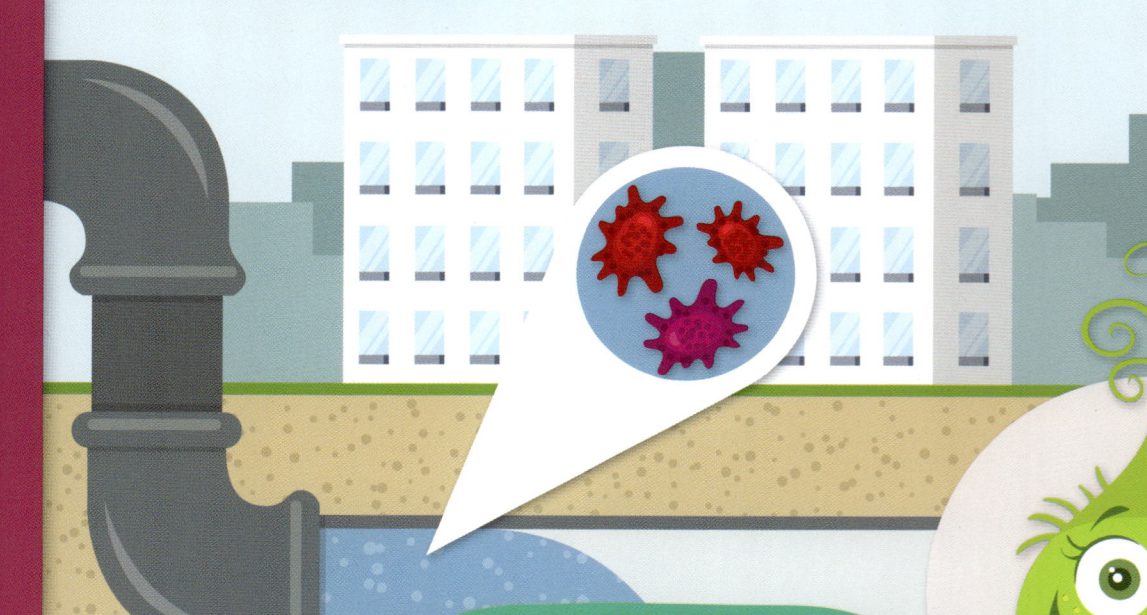

Drinking water is cleaned before it is sent to our taps.

This makes it safe to drink.

Good vs. Bad

While some germs can make us sick, many germs around us can be helpful. Here are two ways how.

Food

Some germs are found in food, such as yogurt and bread. These germs help our bodies work properly.

Medicine

Good germs can keep us from getting sick. **Vaccines** are full of germs that teach our bodies how to fight illnesses.

The germs around us are small, but they can do some big things!

23

Glossary

bacterium a tiny living thing that can make you sick or keep you healthy

cold a common type of illness that can cause sneezing, coughing, and a fever

fungus a plantlike living thing that can't make its own food

spread to move over and cover a bigger distance or area

surface the outside part or layer of something, such as the top of a table

survive to stay alive

vaccines types of medicine that protect people against specific illnesses

virus a tiny germ that can make our bodies sick

Index